BREAKING THE JINX OF FACEBOOK MARKETING CHALLENGES AND GENERATING MASSIVE TRAFFICS & SALES

PRACTICAL STRATEGIES TO ENGAGE AUDIENCE IN FACEBOOK MARKETPLACE

By
EMILE MARTIN

TABLE OF CONTENTS

INTRODUCTION

Do you think it's difficult to promote your company on Facebook at all? Are the outcomes frustrating you? Would you want to discover the most typical Facebook obstacles and discover how to go beyond them? Many of the company owners I deal with find it difficult to use Facebook to its full potential.

I recently carried out a poll to get to the bottom of the problem and decided to share with you some techniques that will help overcome the challenges in the article below in order to get a true understanding of why this is. We gathered information from social media marketing entrepreneurs for this book, which lists many of these difficulties along with some recommended solutions. Among the most notable are:

1.Lack of Adequate Facebook Marketing plan
2. Not Generating Traffic and Leads

3. Not Generating Sales From Facebook

4. Not Effectively Utilizing Dark Posts to Your Advantage For Facebook

CHAPTER 1: LACK OF ADEQUATE FACEBOOK MARKETING PLAN

Facebook is always changing, and user behaviour is too. Facebook has changed over the last five years from what it was. The same is true for clients and users. Social media marketers and managers must always come up with fresh strategies for drawing in new clients and keeping hold of existing ones. They encounter several difficulties along the way.

Given that Facebook is the most popular social media platform for companies to advertise their goods on, it's critical to understand the potential issues with Facebook marketing (as well as solutions).

As an enthusiastic business owner, you want to make sure that you provide your company with the most chance to reach the appropriate audience. You now confront different kinds of obstacles as a result of new means of getting your message out. Facebook marketing is one of those novel endeavours that, when executed skillfully, may yield remarkable outcomes for your company.

Defining Particular Facebook Marketing Objectives

Setting objectives is the first step in using Facebook marketing to accomplish them. This will assist you in creating campaign-centered activities and concentrating your marketing efforts on your intended market. The next stage is to list the precise objectives you want to accomplish. Here, we concentrate on the behaviours you would want your avatar to do upon discovering you and your company on Facebook.

This is a sample list of some important objectives:

❖ X number of people to read your blog each month

❖ Increase email list size each month by X number of subscribers

❖ Offer X spots on coaching programs for sale.

❖ Using email marketing campaigns, create X new Facebook management inquiries each month.

❖ Increase my following by X per month.

It's simple to move to the next level and organize your content, lead magnets, promotions, and blogging strategy to spread your message and strike up conversations with the relevant individuals on Facebook after you have these objectives mapped out and you know who you are talking to.

Here's where you'll see a difference—even in your perception of your Facebook presence. You need the time to carry out your strategy now that you have one. The survey answers above demonstrate that another significant issue that individuals encounter is a lack of time. These practical time-savers might be helpful:

- Make a schedule for your blog and facebook posts' material.
- Give yourself at least 12 weeks to plan your email marketing campaigns.
- Schedule, monitor, and choose viral material using social media platforms. Set up time each week in your calendar to carry out your goals. It may seem easy, but making this positive move really helps.

I advise you to engage someone to do this task for you or with you if you lack the time to accomplish it all. Patience and time are needed for marketing.

Any kind of marketing, whether it be social media, offline, or online, begins with a solid strategy. A Facebook marketing strategy guarantees that you may present your brand's offerings to the appropriate audience. It also helps in the definition of your desired outcomes or goals for your Facebook marketing campaign.

You definitely need a marketing strategy if you want to compete on Facebook with more than 70 million companies. To create a marketing strategy, you must do the following two things: You must be aware of what is effective if you want to succeed on Facebook. This is a short list of the essential components of your plan:

Target market Avatar

Recognize your Facebook target audience. It won't work well to try to get in touch with everyone who could be interested in purchasing your goods and services. Give precise details about the characteristics of your ideal client. Their location and age are simply too much. I advise you to take a seat, draw up a list of the characteristics of your ideal client, give them a name, and describe their general way of life as well as the difficulties they are facing in their line of work.

Making Personas for Customers

Knowing who you are marketing to the target market for whom you developed your goods and brand and who is likely to be interested in and buy them is crucial. In order to do this, you must go into the details of your ideal client, including their demographics, what kind of person they would be if you spoke with them about your products, and what their income should be.

SELECTING APPROPRIATE GOALS TO IMPROVE YOUR OUTCOME

Companies are aware that they must set objectives, but which goals are they most eager to achieve? This has always piqued my curiosity.

Most of my clients naturally desire to see more sales, but they often are unaware of the prerequisites that must be met in order to achieve those sales. Since you are undoubtedly aware that people prefer doing business with individuals they know, like, and trust, let's examine how to choose the appropriate improvement targets and what will happen if you succeed. Three things must be done if you really want to boost sales on Facebook:

- ❖ Put your material in front of the appropriate audience.
- ❖ By fostering a connection with them via your content and weekly mailings, you may gain their trust.
- ❖ Offer solutions that will address their issues. Consequently, this will raise your earnings.

Prior to concentrating on boosting sales, I advise you to give the following your full attention in the following order:

I. Composing the greatest possible blog posts
II. Making eye-catching lead magnets
III. Using Facebook advertisements to increase website traffic
IV. Using Facebook advertisements to expand your email list
V. Increasing interaction with images and videos

LACK OF A CONTENT STRATEGY AS A FACEBOOK MARKETING PROBLEM

Whatever sort of advertisement you decide on, content is crucial to marketing. It must exist whether it is text-based, visual, or audio-based. More significantly, the material you produce must align with your brand's values and Facebook marketing objectives. All things considered, content-free marketing is ineffective. Selling an experience on Facebook is equally as important as selling a product.

Finding out what sort of content is most effective for your brand should be your first priority. A set Facebook business page marketing approach does not exist. How can you avoid this? You may get comprehensive insights on the postings that are most effective for your brand and the reactions that they get from your audience by using Facebook Insights. As an alternative, you may utilize that data to assist you with a social media reporting program.

Planning material for at least 10 to 12 weeks ahead of time is advised. A Facebook content calendar that lists every piece of material you want to post on your page may be made. Investing in social media publishing tools that enables you to plan material far in advance may help you save time. This will also address the issue of determining the best times to publish your material. You may monitor the performance of your postings using the built-in analytics tool included in the majority of this software.

CHAPTER 2: NOT GENERATING TRAFFIC AND LEADS

Because Facebook updates its algorithm often, advertisers struggle to generate enough interest in the material they are providing. Another important factor in this is the kind of user activity.

The leads don't convert even if marketers put a lot of effort into producing excellent content. This may be the result of Facebook beginning to prioritize material from sponsored advertisements. It can also be the result of poorly tailored material for your intended audience. So how would you go about conquering this obstacle?

Enhancing Click-Through Percentage
Right now, organic content is not popular, especially on Facebook. It follows that you must

invest in sponsored advertisements. When making Facebook advertising, some things to keep in mind are

- Select the appropriate ad type for your goal.
- Remain clear and uncomplicated.
- A four-word headline and a fifteen-word description are the ideal lengths.
- Make use of visual materials like pictures
- Test out Facebook Live to improve the content.
- A/B material on a regular basis
- Choosing the Correct Content Mix

As was previously said, you must ascertain the kind of material that would appeal to your target market the most. Selecting between text-based and graphic material is not necessary in this case. It's also important to recognize the kinds of postings that will interest and engage your audience. Does your target market anticipate promotional material, quick social customer service, video tutorials, or educational blog posts?

MAKING USE OF A SPECIFIC LANDING PAGE

This is a crucial strategy for getting leads for your business. When you are running Facebook advertisements, you must have a landing page up. This landing page may get all of the traffic that comes from your adverts. You may then begin nurturing your leads to get quality conversions. One of the following techniques may be used to investigate this combination:

- ➤ Competitions Email-gated material
- ➤ Freebies Coupons
- ➤ Making Use of Facebook Targeting Features

It is not advisable to launch your website blindly and hope for the best. Both money and time are being wasted. Reaching the specialized audience for your company is possible with Facebook's extensive targeting possibilities.

Facebook Targeting Options

On Facebook, there are three methods you may contact and target your consumers.

Principal Audience

For this kind of audience, you will need to manually go through Facebook's available filters and choose the ones that correspond with your target audience's personalities. Demographics, geography, hobbies, conduct, and relationships are some of these criteria. To achieve your marketing objectives, you may make it as wide or as narrow as you choose.

Particular Audience

These are the individuals you want to connect with on Facebook, but you already know outside of the platform. This choice may help you close deals more quickly while also fortifying your relationships with consumers. Facebook gives you many options for reaching these individuals.

After you've established a Facebook custom audience, you may configure your advertising to only appear to them.

Audience Members Who Look Like
By using this option, you may increase the size of your target market without significantly changing the kind of customers you have identified for your business. These are folks who have potential to become leads or make purchases and who are comparable to your specialized audience.

NO ROI ON FACEBOOK MARKETING CAMPAIGNS

The next natural step after running a few Facebook paid ad campaigns is to figure out how to gauge the effectiveness of Facebook ads and their return on investment (ROI). This has proven difficult, not because there is a lot of data and statistics involved, but rather because there isn't a clear relationship between marketing and sales.

Facebook ROI is determined by more than simply how many people like and share your posts. Facebook does an excellent job of giving you comprehensive statistics and reports on the performance of each of your campaigns in relation to the objectives you have set for them. These are the main categories of insights you may utilize and anticipate seeing on Facebook.

Viewer Insights

This provides you with details about the individuals who have connected with you outside of Facebook and the custom audience that follows your brand on Facebook. You will learn about their hobbies, way of life, and demography. With this knowledge, you may eliminate the guesswork involved in marketing and produce content that connects with the audience.

Reports on Advertisements

Similar to Audience Insights, which is used to assess the impact of organic content, AdWords reports provide you with data on the effectiveness of your Facebook advertisements. This aids in your comprehension of the kind of influence your brand has on its consumers and followers. You may enhance your marketing strategies with the help of this knowledge.

You can track the effectiveness of your campaigns and determine if you are using your adverts to target the appropriate demographic. Check to see whether your advertisements are yielding the best results possible; if not, you may need to start again from scratch.

Divided Testing

One of the most important parts of marketing, as previously said, is A/B testing. You must continuously experiment to see what kinds of creativity and content appeal to different audience groups. This enables you to concentrate on the ones that are producing higher returns on investment. One of the greatest social media marketing platforms for companies has been developed by Facebook via significant progress.

And you must make the most of it. Additional Facebook Reporting Choices

You may investigate a plethora of other methods provided by Facebook for reporting purposes, both online and offline. You can monitor which offline events resulted in what sort of sales, track the effectiveness of cross-marketing your goods and services, etc. Visit Facebook's help page to learn all there is to know about it.

FAQs ABOUT FACEBOOK MARKETING ISSUES

What issues arise with Facebook advertising? The following are the top 4 issues with Facebook advertising that you may run into:

1. No Facebook marketing objectives or target client personas.
2. Not understanding what sort of material is best for your company.
3. Fail to generate sufficient interest in your material.

4. Facebook ad ROI measurement is challenging.

Which are some of Facebook's business-related issues?
Among the issues that companies run into with Facebook are:

1. Facebook has a huge user base, making it difficult to target the correct demographic.
2. Facebook lacks complete control and customization.
3. Facebook groups have less control.

What issues does marketing face today?
Some businesses are still having trouble with marketing, even if others are having success, particularly with social media. Occasionally, marketers encounter problems with lead generation, trend detection or worse, trends they miss entirely: tool malfunctions, incapacity to manage and exploit data, and inadequate content creation.

WHAT IS THE MOST DIFFICULT THING ABOUT FACEBOOK ADS?

The cost of Facebook advertisements presents the largest obstacle for the majority of companies. The cost of Facebook advertisements varies based on the nation from which you are attempting to run them. The average cost is $7.19 for 1000 impressions and $0.97 for each click. Additionally, there is a limit on how many individuals see the advertisements. Therefore, the cost may be more if you want the advertisements to reach a wider audience.

CHAPTER 3: NOT GENERATING SALES AND TRAFFICS ON FACEBOOK

Facebook may drive traffic to your website since it is the unchallenged leader in social networking. Given that Facebook accounts for 80.4% of all referrals to eCommerce sites, it's really fairly difficult for it not to. With Facebook owning Instagram coming in second place with 10.7%. Therefore, Facebook is the place to go if you're seeking a technique to increase your revenue.

I must emphasize that these recommendations take time to take impact, just like it takes time for a website to turn a profit. You shouldn't anticipate a sharp rise in revenues over night. It just will not occur.

Examine Your Market and Business

When it comes to Facebook marketing, you must take your audience into account. To get the desired outcomes, you may need to use various techniques and methods depending on the audience and kind of company.

For instance, do you own a small company that also sells goods online, or do you just have an eCommerce website? When you own a small company, your main goal is usually to get customers in for in-person visits as well as online transactions.

And you would be promoting locally in that scenario. On the other hand, an eCommerce website may be promoted to everyone, anywhere in the world. As such, the methods you use will vary.

This also holds true for the people that make up your target market. Advertising to young people should be done quite differently than to older audiences. To get the finest outcomes, you must be aware of this.

Fortunately, if done properly, there is a good chance that your message will reach the intended recipient because of the vast number of Facebook's audience.

ELEVEN SCIENTIFICALLY PROVEN REASONS YOUR FACEBOOK MARKETING ISN'T BRINGING IN ANY BUSINESS ENQUIRIES OR SALES

Given that 3 million people in Singapore use Facebook, the thought of promoting your goods or services online may seem like a really interesting strategy. This represents an astounding 55% of Singapore's population! A marketing strategy that's too wonderful to pass up is reaching more than half of Singapore's population. In Singapore, a lot of companies use or have attempted to use Google SEM and Facebook marketing.

Regretfully, a lot of them claim that the platform isn't generating much revenue for them. Fear not there is still hope, and you can take some action to increase sales on Facebook.

We'll show you 11 scientific reasons why you're not receiving consumer inquiries or purchases from Facebook marketing, based on our experience helping companies routinely produce $250,000 in sales each month using Facebook marketing alone.

1. Bad images
2. You're overselling
3. You're not interacting with your audience.
4You don't have a likeable personality on your Facebook profile.
5. Your offerings are just insufficiently good.
6. You're failing to communicate your USP (unique selling proposition)
7. There's no evidence or proof
8. Uninteresting headlines
9. Your rivals are more adept at it.
10. No one would purchase your good or service online
11. You don't use Facebook advertising

1. Bad images

It's becoming more and more popular to use eye-catching photos and videos in your social media marketing strategy, but having high-quality photographs on your Facebook profile is crucial.

Using subpar images while communicating on Facebook represents the kind of experience prospective buyers may have with the product or service. In fact, consumers in certain sectors place more value on a product or service's image than on its reviews or rating. Posts with images are clicked on three times more often than those with only text.

It has been shown that superior photos and videos boost conversions by more than 80%. They are also a terrific technique to leave a lasting impression and will help your business stand out from the cacophonous internet throng.

Check out Facebook's current course if you're not persuaded yet. One of their advertising restrictions is that your advertisements must use more than 20% text. This demonstrates Facebook's desire to maintain its visual platform. Our busy environment is another reason why well-designed images are superior. Every minute, information is thrown at us. Visitors won't be very interested in your lengthy text postings or dull images. A picture says a thousand words, as the saying goes. How accurate.

2. You're overselling

It's illegal to oversell on your Facebook page. Consumers don't want to be sold to all the time; this is something they have to deal with all day, and you don't want to make things worse. We are exposed to 3,000 advertisements per day on average, according to study. Wow, so many advertisements. There isn't much focus on us.

Ads are starting to blind us. Rather, your company should use inbound marketing techniques to attract clients by offering them something of value. One of the best ways to get their attention and keep them interested long enough to desire to purchase from you is to provide value in the form of information or even entertainment.

Not that you shouldn't market to your clients. I'm simply suggesting that you should put more of an emphasis on educating your clients since, in this day and age, we are constantly exposed to advertisements. Your clientele is becoming more astute. They make comparisons between items before making a purchase. Education, not sales, is what consumers need to hear.

You know your industry inside and out. Make use of this. Make use of your expertise to inform and interest your clients. You conquer when you educate. You establish credibility. Customers will appreciate your company and the goods and services you provide, and you'll have their attention.

3. *You aren't conversing with your viewers.*

As in every partnership, there must be mutual communication. The opinions of your consumers are equally as significant as your company and what you have to say.

A key engagement goal is to give your clients the impression that they are valued, significant, and that your company cares about them. Likes, shares, and comments are the many ways that users interact on Facebook. There are three distinct approaches to engaging your Facebook followers with your business.

While likes and shares can help your company boost your organic reach and exposure, the purpose of Facebook comments is to hear what your followers have to say. To foster interaction with your Facebook followers, your company should think about using engagement strategies like polls, quizzes, and competitions in addition to posting news and current events relevant to your industry.

4. You don't have a likeable personality on your Facebook profile.

People do, in fact, relate to one another. They have nothing to do with faceless, impersonal companies. Take a look at the major brands. Every company, from Nike to Ikea, has a likeable personality that emotionally connects with its customers.

You need to establish a likeable presence on your Facebook profile if you want people to remember you. The first step to selling to clients is to be in the forefront of their minds. Consumers like companies that are relevant, genuine, and real. It is neither fun nor memorable to be boring.

People want to be understood. In what ways does your company show compassion for its clients? Being aware of the issues and demands of your clients will enable you to develop a brand persona that they will value in their life,

much like a friend. Customers will remain loyal
to you if they can recall your brand. The sales
you need from them will come from their
loyalty.

5. Your offerings are just insufficiently good.

Sometimes, purchases just don't happen,
regardless of how effectively your Facebook
profile and advertisements are done. It's possible
that your goods and services are subpar. They
are unnecessary, or your rivals provide superior
goods and services. Do you provide goods that
are superior to those of your rivals? In
comparison to your rivals, are you providing
your clients with more value?

Note: Just because your items are less expensive
than those of your rivals doesn't imply that you
are providing more value to your clients. Value
for money is what customers seek for, not the
cheapest goods.

Does your offering address a problem? Excellent goods and services provide a solution. It's more difficult to market to customers if your goods or services don't address their problems. It's not needed right now. It's not a necessity; it's a desire. Do you aggressively promote the fact that your goods and services alleviate problems on your Facebook page?

It's hard to obtain sales from any marketing efforts if your company doesn't convey this important message, even if it provides the finest priced goods or services. There are two easy methods that you may convey this important information on your Facebook page:

Pinned posts with cover photos are the two paramount things they will glance at first When a consumer visits your Facebook page.

6. You're failing to communicate your USP (unique selling point).

It's likely that there are a lot of rivals in your industry, making it difficult for you to stand apart. Communicating your USP will assist your audience choose to purchase from you rather than your rivals and will help you stand out from the competition. 3 requirements should be met by your USP:

Is your USP genuine? For instance, the town's cheapest furniture shop. Is this assertion accurate?
Is it relevant to your intended audience? Do they care about it?
Is it possible to be proven?
Consumers don't have time to look far and wide for your business's unique selling proposition.
Put it at the forefront of your Facebook page.

7. There's no evidence or proof

Customers have only fifteen seconds to see your Facebook page after landing on it. In that period, you have to convince clients of your product's legitimacy.

Its believability is based on evidence. In Singapore, advertising has a negative reputation. A lot of people get conned. Singaporeans are becoming more doubtful. If you don't have any evidence, customers won't purchase from you. Your Facebook page is your on-call salesperson, in our opinion. A salesperson that works for you around-the-clock needs evidence in order to close deals.

Visitors to your Facebook page are welcome at any time. They can decide not to give you a call to ask questions about your offerings. They may not provide you an opportunity to clarify. It is also important that you incorporate evidence in your Facebook posts, visuals, and content to demonstrate to potential clients why they should believe in you and make a purchase. Customer testimonials, before-and-after pictures, celebrity endorsements, research support, product demonstrations, and many other formats may all be used as proof.

8. Uninteresting headlines

Aside from a visually arresting photograph, what is the first thing you notice when you go through your news feed on Facebook or any other platform? Fantastic headline! If the title of your Facebook post fails to grab the attention of the majority of people, they will just scroll down their page. Take some time to come up with ideas for headlines before publishing your material.

Make sure your headlines pique readers' interest so they will click through to your page to learn more. See this page for tips on crafting effective headlines.

9. *Your rivals are more adept at it.*

Customers are becoming more knowledgeable every day. Information is more accessible than ever thanks to review websites like TripAdvisor, Hardwarezone, HungryGoWhere, Facebook pages, and a ton of websites in your specialties. Customers are able to locate what they're looking for. Product quality, pricing, corporate reputation, and a host of other factors.

Prior to purchasing, customers investigate products. They will never deviate from what they believe to be right. The harsh reality may be that your items are not superior to those of your rivals if clients are not purchasing from you despite your best efforts. Keep an eye on your rivals and emulate their actions. Do they have a better offer than you do?

How can you better serve your customers? To be competitive and guarantee that you are always providing your clients with a superior deal, you should constantly keep up with your rivals.

10. No one would purchase your goods or services online

Even though almost anything may be purchased online in today's rapidly evolving technological world, there are still situations in which it is impractical to offer a specific item or service online.

For instance, a guy wants to propose to his girlfriend and is searching the internet for an engagement ring. He has $5,000 in his budget. Even though he may spend a lot of time perusing the internet, it is unlikely that he would buy the ring without first seeing it in person. There are a lot of such situations when it is improbable to make an internet purchase.

If your goods or services go under this category, you should concentrate on directing leads to your physical store rather than aiming for internet sales. Consider strategies to get customers inside your business, such as offering

a one-time discount voucher that they may
redeem at the counter.

11. *You don't advertise on Facebook.*

You believed that you might generate revenue
without having to spend any money? Even if this
could be the most advantageous course of action,
it might not be feasible. Facebook has evolved
into a pay-for-play website.

The organic reach on Facebook is gone.

Research indicates that organic reach reaches a
mere 2% of your followers. Not bad for so many
supporters. Even Facebook sites with over
100,000 admirers find that this is not a big
enough number; how about tiny companies with
just 1,000 fans? It's essential to invest in
Facebook advertising. Above all, it has a very
high positive return on investment. For a very
low cost, Facebook advertising enables you to
target consumers who are interested in your kind

of goods or services. View the Facebook marketing outcomes of one of our clients.

Using a $1,500 ad purchase, he reached 227,135 individuals. The click-through rate was a mere $0.12. You know what happened to this local retailer's sales? $37,000. What is the return on investment? an astounding 2466%. You cannot accomplish a ROI of 2466% with the majority of other marketing methods. With search engine marketing, this specific client's average return on investment was a mere 153%.

Naturally, we're not claiming that every customer will have these kinds of outcomes. Numerous elements influence it. But with Facebook marketing initiatives, the majority of our customers see a significant increase in return on investment. Examine your offerings and what has to be changed after taking into account the reasons why customers aren't purchasing from you on Facebook.

We can assure you of increased sales since we have a proven track record of successfully managing Facebook ads for our customers.

SEVEN WAYS TO INCREASE FACEBOOK SALES AND TRAFFICS ON YOUR FACEBOOK MARKETING SPACE

Increase Sales

Because each website is different, the outcomes might differ too. The article will examine the top 7 strategies for increasing Facebook sales. But it's crucial to keep in mind that the more active you are on Facebook, the more successful you will be.

Add Facebook Connectivity to Your Website

It makes sense for your website to be linked to social media platforms if you want to have a presence there. There are several methods available for integrating Facebook with your website, particularly if WordPress is being used.

Here are a few of the most well-liked methods for incorporating Facebook into your website:

Facebook Share Button: By clicking on a share button, a visitor may tell their friends about your sites or items on Facebook. In essence, it allows your visitors to advertise on your behalf. Furthermore, it seems better when a third party links to your items without receiving payment.

Facebook Like Button: With a like button, users can easily show their support for you on your website without ever going to Facebook. This significantly raises the likelihood of receiving a like. This is significant since your Facebook page will become more visible the more likes it receives.

Facebook Login: By enabling users to log in using their Facebook credentials, you may assist visitors in creating an account on your website. This offers two benefits: 1) users may establish accounts more quickly and easily; and 2) it gives you the chance to get likes or follows during the registration process.

Facebook Messenger: Facebook Messenger is the most sensible option for companies looking to enable consumer conversation on their websites. There are already close to 2 billion users, and in a few years, that number is predicted to rise to around 3 billion. Adding it to a website is simple.

Facebook Pixel: With the help of this technology, you can track consumer behavior as they engage with your advertising on Facebook. You can observe, for instance, whether someone clicked on your advertisement and then made a purchase. It will become more intelligent and ensure that the individuals your advertisements target are more inclined to do certain behaviours.

Post to Facebook From WordPress: If you post on Facebook often, it may take a while to finish. Posting straight from your WordPress website will cut down on the amount of time it takes.

This may also help you avoid distractions whilst working, since you won't have to access Facebook at all. There might be a long list of methods to incorporate Facebook into your website. That may really make a nice story on its own. However, the goal is to make sure that your website offers a means for users to engage with Facebook.

2. Share videos on Facebook.
After-Video Content

The most watched material on Facebook or any other social media platform, really is videos. Compared to other post types, videos have a user engagement rate of 59% higher. Moreover, videos made up 81.8% of the top 500 Facebook postings in 2018.

The increase in smartphone usage over time is mostly to blame for this. The amount of mobile video that is consumed increases by almost 100% annually. As you can understand, if this pattern keeps up, you won't have any say in the subject of video marketing.

The largest error, however, is to limit your Facebook post to only videos. Rather, each video needs to contain supplementary text providing extra information and connecting viewers to your website. This increases the likelihood that someone will visit your website right away after seeing a video.

Remember that the content of videos is also evolving. You may benefit from the significant advancements that live video content has been making in the future by using Facebook Live. This increases engagement and purchases by letting viewers connect with you live!

3. Enhance Your Facebook Page With A Store
This is maybe the easiest and most apparent technique to increase sales on Facebook. Nonetheless, it is still worthwhile. Additionally, it is among the most effective strategies to turn a new Facebook visitor into a client. But you can't just add a business to any old Facebook page.

You could, but it won't be warmly received. Rather, in order to succeed in any way with this, you must ensure that your Facebook profile seems reliable. This is very significant. A website that seems to have been put up at the last minute will not inspire confidence in potential customers. This implies that you need a profile picture, cover photo, customer reviews that are public, and more. Asking yourself whether you would buy anything from this shop is a solid rule of thumb. You can usually infer what the other person(s) would think if you say no.

That being said, this isn't limited to your Facebook profile. Since every transaction will be done on your own website, you can easily predict what will happen if you go from a high-quality Facebook shop to a dubious-looking website. Online, appearances count, so dress well!

4. Launch Exclusive Offers & Deals on Facebook

A tried-and-true strategy for increasing Facebook sales is to provide exclusive offers, deals, discounts, freebies, or whatever you want to call them. Customers will find it beneficial to follow your Facebook account as a result.

And the more followers you have, the more like it is that someone will purchase something especially at a discount!

The way you distribute unique offers and bargains, however, is crucial. Is it possible, for instance, for someone who simply happened across your page to benefit from the offer? Or should it go to someone who likes and is following your page? It is obvious that visitors that engage with your Facebook page are more valuable, and as such, they need to be given something in return. Making it mandatory for someone to tag a certain number of friends is one of the best strategies to increase your following. This may start a domino effect that swiftly increases the number of followers on your profile.

5. *Advertisements on Facebook*

Make Advertising Campaigns
It should come as no surprise that Facebook advertising is included in a list of advice on how to boost Facebook sales, since almost everyone is aware of their potential. It's reasonable to assume that not many websites can match the social media behemoth, with its monthly viewership of 2.5 billion users.

However, Facebook's extensive user data collection is what gives its advertisements such potency. This makes it possible for the advertisements to be shown to highly precise audiences, which makes it a very efficient method of advertising delivery. It is important to note that Facebook advertising is not free, in contrast to the other suggestions on this list. Also, the additional expense might be prohibitive for a newly launched website or company. On the other hand, there are several choices for price. Actually, you could start a Facebook marketing campaign for as low as $5 a day. Additionally, you may start paying more to get better outcomes as soon as you see the advertising begin to function and bring in money.

6. Promote client testimonials

It seems fantastic for companies to have nice comments and reviews all over your Facebook selling page. Not to mention that over ninety-five percent of consumers read internet reviews, you can see how crucial favourable ones are.

The most important issue is, of course, how to encourage people to post encouraging comments on my Facebook profile. First of all, you have to activate a feature called Recommendations directly from Facebook. This adds a new tab to your page where users may post recommendations or reviews while signed in to Facebook. But just turning it on won't cause every follower to post a review right now.

To add a little incentive, several establishments will sometimes give customers a discount code off their next purchase if they submit a review. There are several strategies for promoting reviews. But, being kind and writing a little note with a link after checkout may really help.

7. Promote Products in Your Posts
Display Your Products
Of course, the most important thing is to make sure you are publishing often in order to draw in new followers and maintain your current ones. You've just really benefited from your ability to effectively create postings regarding your items that are also interesting.

Let's take the scenario where you offer gaming gear. While playing a new game, you may write a post on how comfy your new headset is. This highlights the fact that a headset you offer is comfy and gives you the opportunity to tell them a little bit about yourself.

This might vary greatly depending on the kind of product you offer. For example, creating content for food, cars, and fashion is simpler than creating content for underwater basket weaving. You may simply increase sales by making sure that the products in your postings are highlighted.

Examine Alternative Platforms
Alternative Social Media Channels
Although Facebook is undoubtedly the dominant social media site, it is not the only one. You must expand to new platforms if you want to increase your website's sales. Other sites you should think about using for marketing are YouTube, Pinterest, Instagram, Twitter, and Instagram.

Look up any significant firm on any number of social media sites in a few minutes. You need to notice right away that they are present on the majority of them. These businesses have devoted marketing teams that work to ensure that they are seen, and you should too.

You probably don't have the same resources as you had before. However, actively managing numerous social media accounts is totally achievable with a little work and perhaps a little less sleep. It's important to diversify in this situation.

Only the Beginning
Increasing Facebook sales is certain with the advice on this list. That said, the procedure will take some time to complete. Many of these techniques won't start to show results for weeks or even months. However, everyone must begin somewhere. A Facebook sales channel is an effective tool for entrepreneurs, so don't hesitate to start using it. Your revenue will increase at a faster rate the sooner you get started.

I discussed some of the main obstacles that business owners have when using Facebook marketing in the beginning of this book. Naturally, generating revenue is a recurring subject, and that makes sense, right?

Once again, a lot of the business owners I know put a lot of effort into producing excellent content for their sites; users like it and interact with it, but sales aren't happening.

We should all post two kinds of material on Facebook, in my opinion, depending on our brand and how customers engage with us and our company.
Remember that some pages have extremely involved and active fans, while other pages have admirers who are either very active email subscribers or blog readers but don't participate with the page directly.

Natural Content
For the most part, I don't pay Facebook to promote my organic material. To engage a segment of my fan base, I generate and curate material using Canva, Picmonkey, and Postplanner.

I interact with my followers via organic material to amuse, inspire, and learn a little bit more about them. If I don't get to see all of my admirers, I won't go crazy and stop sleeping. Generally speaking, a sizable chunk of my fan base responds when I choose very high-quality material.

Examples of content that is organic:

- Asking probing questions
- Inspirational sayings
- Behind-the-scenes business photos
- Purchased Content

It's critical to see Facebook as a sales funnel if you want to use the network to boost sales. This is where Facebook advertisements come into play, and by doing this, you may begin using Facebook to boost sales.

Please note that your efforts will be in vain unless you have something that someone really needs or wants, regardless of how skilled we are at creating Facebook advertising.

We must provide a solution based on the issues that we are aware of facing our target, raise awareness via our marketing initiatives, and keep gaining the confidence of our fans, blog readers, and subscribers.

Instances of material that is paid for:

- ★ Create a lead magnet promotion post in dark mode.
- ★ Encourage weekly blog posts and build a specific audience for your website so you can target them later.
- ★ Facebook promotions for nearby businesses' services, such as hair salons and eateries
- ★ Facebook page competitions

COMMON TRAVERSES

I was curious as to what was preventing company owners from utilizing Facebook to their advantage. Was it due to a lack of understanding, conviction, tactic, or anything else?

I think a lot of business owners have trouble arranging their Facebook ad expenditures because they don't know how to prioritize their spending and don't know whether their investment is yielding a profit.

Perhaps Facebook marketing isn't the correct move for you and your company right now if you really don't have the money, time, or resources to dedicate to it. I do, however, have a question: Can you afford to make no investments in your company? Here are a few more remarks from those who responded to this query:

Despite my limited resources, I want what I have to work, but I'm not sure where to begin or how to go about it.
I procrastinate for so long that it prevents me from going ahead.
I'd want to know how to best use my money on Facebook in order to get results rather than spending it in a local newspaper, where I now have no idea how to distribute funds to my team.

CHAPTER 4: ON UTILIZING FACEBOOK DARK POST

I was getting ready for work one morning when I did my routine social media scan and when I was going through Facebook, I started to see advertisements for businesses I didn't remember following. For example, I don't follow the B2B firm Drift's Facebook page, but I read their blog quite a bit. But I still saw this advertisement:

Facebook sponsored post from Drift
Despite the fact that this surprised me, I wasn't really concerned since I assumed, partially accurately, that my online activity had affected the kinds of advertisements I was seeing. But I couldn't locate the advertisement I saw above when I went to the corporate Page to follow it. That's when I started to wonder: How can an advertisement that shows up in my main feed not display on the page of that company?

Subsequently, I understood what was happening: the advertisement I had seen was a dark post. Dark articles target audiences with the express purpose of generating leads and converting them. We'll talk about dark posts on Facebook next, so don't panic if you've never heard of them.

What Are the Content Dark Posts?

There might be some misunderstanding when discussing dark postings on what they are and how they work. For example, they are completely distinct from dark social and are seen by many channels as sponsored advertisements. Let's define a dark post so that everyone can see the whole picture.

A dark post: what is it?
Unlike boosted and organic posts, a dark post is a targeted advertisement that doesn't show up on the advertiser's timeline or in the feeds of their followers. Rather, dark posts which are often

identified as sponsored content appear on the feeds of the audiences who are being targeted.

For instance, even though I don't follow Squarespace on Facebook, the firm nonetheless sent me a targeted advertisement, perhaps because some of the people Squarespace wants to reach are represented in my trackable online behaviour:

Facebook targeted ad for Squarespace
This message seems to be an ordinary advertisement from a website I follow on my news feed. However, the advertisement isn't present when I go to visit the corporate website. This post is deemed "dark" as the advertisement itself doesn't display on the corporate page and instead shows up on the timeline of an audience member who doesn't follow the page.

The expression "dark social," which refers to social media traffic that cannot be identified by social media analytics, should not be confused with dark postings.

Dark posting may be a useful strategy if you want to interact with more audience members and appear on their feed with a targeted advertisement. The fact that the material is still an advertisement gives you more control over what your target audience sees. The content of the advertisement may also be customized to introduce your business, explain what it stands for, and be created with lead generation in mind.

While dark posts often have the same characteristics everywhere, let's talk about how things vary a little bit on Facebook.

Facebook Shadow Posts: An Explanation
Facebook dark posts are distinct from those you may come across on other social networking platforms; in fact, they go by a different name.

What is a dark post on Facebook?
A Facebook dark post, also known as an "Unpublished Page," is an advertisement that appears on the feeds of certain consumers rather

than the advertiser's Business Page or feed right away. Ad Manager is where you may create these adverts and choose the distribution method.

Additionally, they provide more effective A/B testing outcomes by enabling you to test advertisements with consumers who have previously engaged with your brand before distributing them to new audiences.

You may choose which audiences and how often posts are shown with dark posts, so you can be sure that no unsuitable adverts for converted leads will be shown to them. They are targeted advertisements, but they are shown to a different and more focused audience. It is more under your hands to decide what kinds of postings your prospects view. You have control over the advertisement's visibility, scheduling, and inclusion in promotions within a broader set when you make a dark post.

By now, you're undoubtedly aware that although dark posts could seem a bit contentious, viewers may consider them as sly advertisements rather than tailored advertising experiences. Because of this, Facebook has modified many aspects of dark posts (as well as Facebook advertisements in general) since their launch in an attempt to maintain transparency:

Posts that are dark are labelled. Even though they don't necessarily have a conventional ad appearance, Facebook dark posts are always identified as sponsored content. The most significant change is that viewers can now identify which company postings on all Facebook-owned social media networks (including Instagram) are advertisements.
The Advertising Collection Through browsing their Ad Library, audiences may choose whether they are viewing dark posts. Entering a firm's name in the search bar of the Ad Library allows users to see all of the advertising the company is running on Facebook. Additionally, they have

the option to filter these adverts based on reach, activity, audience, and relevancy:

Facebook Ad Library Example

The Ad Library may be accessed by a user in two ways: first, by URL. You may start searching by typing facebook.com/ads/library if you're already on Facebook. The right sidebar will include a "Page Transparency" section if you are on the company's particular page:

transparency of pages

When you choose "See More," a page with further information about the business, including its founding year and key connections, will open. You may see the firm's Ad Library by clicking on the box at the bottom of the page, which indicates whether or not the company is running ads:

Using Facebook's Ad Library from the Page section This box also provides information on the kind of advertisements the business runs, helping viewers determine whether or not they are really viewing an advertisement.

After learning about dark posts, their audience interactions, and their uses, let's go on to discussing how to create them.

Facebook Dark Posting Techniques
There isn't much that separates publishing a dark post on Facebook from generating a different kind of ad. We'll go over everything you need to know in depth and provide optimization advice.

If you want a more thorough guide on running Facebook ads in general, you can check out another one of our blogs.

1. To see your posts, go to Ads Manager.
You will first go to Facebook Ads Manager. You're undoubtedly used to this feature if you've previously utilized Facebook advertisements. If not, consider Facebook's Ad Manager tool to be your main hub for running advertisements on Facebook and other Facebook-owned properties.

To use Ads Manager, click the drop-down menu in the upper left corner, as seen below:

Getting to postings on Facebook with Ad Manager
The next step is to choose the "Page Posts" option, which is the second option under the Ads Manager area. This subsection is located under "Create & Manage."

2. Set up your post that is dark.
You'll then be brought to the screen that has your dark postings. You will see any previously published Page Posts here, whether they are planned, published, or unpublished.

The only thing you can do if you don't already have any Page Posts is make one, so click that button to get going! This screen will appear after:

Making a Facebook Unpublished Page Post
You may have selected the incorrect action if "Create Unpublished Page Post" isn't shown at

the top. Recall that the only method to dark post on Facebook is via unpublished pages.

You can then complete your advertisement's information from here. Remember that selecting the first option, "Only use this post for an ad," would prevent the post from being published to your corporate Page, which is what you want. Eventually, the second choice will be shown on your Page.

3. Choose or build your target audiences.
In this area, former Facebook Ads Manager users may choose their pre-segmented ad packages. For those who are unfamiliar, you may build audience segments when you launch a campaign:

Facebook ad targeting: Take note of how detailed you may be in your audience segmentation by incorporating factors like age, gender, geography, language, interests, and behaviours. These choices were made to assist you in reaching the audiences most likely to relate to your communications.

By selecting Ads Manager > Audiences > Create Audience > Custom Audiences > Facebook Page from the drop-down box, you may reach this page. After that, a suggestion to build and segment audiences will appear:

How to choose a Facebook custom audience 4. Make your dark post more effective.

You may optimize your article after you're satisfied with it. We'll discuss a few practical optimization pointers here. See our comprehensive guide on Facebook marketing for a more in-depth look at Facebook ad optimization.

I will be discussing what I have lovingly named "The Three R's of Quick Optimization." Run, Review, and Resize are them.

Conduct an A/B experiment. First, examine the outcomes of any A/B testing you've already done and consider how you may use them for your new dark article. Perhaps certain content struck a chord with readers more than others, or perhaps they were simply drawn to a particular one. You may choose the best method for contacting new prospects by consulting your current clientele.

Examine the Ad metrics Open the program for social media analytics. Ad management software may only be available via Facebook's analytics tool or through an external tool such as a CRM. You may decide which ad elements to optimize for a higher return on investment (ROI), such as including a call-to-action (CTA) button to boost conversion rates, when you evaluate your stats. Reduce the size of your audience Resize and reconfigure your viewers if you discover when making your advertisement that they should be taken into consideration. Maybe you've realized that you want to target a smaller audience in a different place. If so, go ahead and build a new audience perhaps with a focus on lead generation via dark posts or modify an existing one.

After that, your dark post, also known as an unpublished page post, will be prepared to appear in lead news feeds and be ready for conversion. You are now familiar with every detail of a Facebook Unpublished Page post. How are you going to take advantage of them?

www.ingramcontent.com/pod-product-compliance
Lightning Source LLC
Chambersburg PA
CBHW050052260726
48658CB00005B/1901